PARKS

A Scenic Guide

Jeanne Broome   SAGUARO AT SUNSET

AN AMERICAN TRAVELER SERIES PUBLICATION

Deborahann Smith

2006 Printing

ISBN 13: 978-1-55838-094-3
ISBN 10: 1-55838-094-9

American Traveler Press
A Division of Primer Publishers
5738 North Central Avenue
Phoenix, Arizona 85012
1-800-521-9221

Cover photo, Chiricahua National Monument, Courtesy Greg Gnesios
Page 41 photo © 1999 Arizona State Parks

Printed in China,
Published in the United States of America

10 9 8 7 6

WELCOME

Publications about Arizona are often written in a lyrical, mystical fashion. It's true that the haunting beauty of this land seems to handle the soul, sculpting it with splendor—as geologic processes over millions of years carved out enormous red canyons, balancing rock formations, and rainbow-colored craters. Have on-lookers always felt so inspired? Possibly not, but the stories and dwellings of early inhabitants have interwoven to make them an integral part of Arizona's parks and monuments.

Humans first lived in Arizona about 11,000 years ago. They hunted and gathered for 7,000 years until maize and squash were introduced through Mexican trade, and people turned to farming. With a more dependable food supply, populations increased and three distinct Indian cultures developed. The Anasazi "dry-farmed" the northern plateau, relying on rain to water their plants. The central mountain Mogollons used simple irrigation techniques. In the south, the Hohokam designed irrigation canals so complex that engineers based modern-day Phoenix systems on them. By the mid-1400s, whole villages moved (possibly due to drought, overpopulation, disease, or warfare) and Navajos and Apaches arrived. Spanish gold-seekers came in 1500, followed later by Anglo explorers. The intermesh of different people created territorial conflict, until resolution made Arizona the peaceful and culture-rich state that it is today.

This guide provides an overview of parks and monuments in Arizona. If you wish to adventure further we suggest the publications from our American Traveler Series (see a list of titles on the back cover) and the Easy Field Guide Series:

Desert Birds

Desert Cactus

Desert Insects

Indian Art and Legends of the Southwest

Invertebrate Fossils of Arizona Mammals of Arizona

Mammals of Arizona

Rock Art Symbols of the Southwest

Southwestern Night Sky

Southwestern Petroglyphs

Southwestern Snakes

Trees of Arizona

Triassic, Jurassic & Cretaceous Reptiles & Dinosaurs of Arizona

Additional titles of interest are listed on our website www.americantravelerpress.com.

CONTENTS

Chiricahua Ntl. Monument   DUCK ON A ROCK

NATIONAL PARKS & MONUMENTS

Encompassing 113,909 miles of dramatic terrain—from scorching deserts to mountains and rivers—Arizona has more parks and monuments than any other state. Some were established to protect the state's diverse plant and wildlife populations. Others take advantage of recreational opportunities that lakes, rivers, and mountains provide. Still others celebrate giant forests (now petrified), where fearsome dinosaurs roamed 225 million years ago. Arizona's fascinating Indian history is told among the multitude of cliff dwellings, cultures more than a thousand years old preserved in national parks and monuments.

National monuments, national parks, national historic sites and national recreation sites in Arizona are managed by the National Park Service or by the Bureau of Land Management. Most areas require an admission fee per vehicle. Park campgrounds range from primitive (cold water pit toilets) to "fancy" (flush toilets, hot showers and laundry facilities) with a comparable range of fees. A "family unit camp site" includes parking space, picnic table, and fireplace or fire pit. Reservations are necessary for higher-use areas. Pets must be leashed and aren't allowed in the backcountry. For more information from the National Park Service visit www.nps.gov. For a Bureau of Land Management contact in Arizona call 602-417-9200. BLM is also online at www.az.blm.gov.

John Beckett

AGUA FRIA

Windy and wild, this National Monument newcomer is characterized by a high semi-desert grassland plateau consisting of two mesas and crossed by the Agua Fria (Spanish for "cold water") River Canyon and its tributaries. Established in 2000, and managed by the Bureau of Land Management, the 71,000-acre monument rises dramatically from a mere 600 feet above sea level in the riverbed to a 4,300-foot elevation in the northern hills.

Between 1250 and 1450 A.D., thousands of people inhabited the area, which contains one of the most significant systems of prehistoric sites in the Southwest. Within the monument are four major pueblo settlements and at least 450 sites including stone-masonry pueblos of 100 rooms or more situated on the edges of steep canyons. There is also an abundance of petroglyphs containing geometric, abstract and animal designs. Petroglyph sites range from single designs on boulders to entire cliffs etched with art. A look around this rich biological community abundant with animals offers a clue of the artists' inspiration. Today's wildlife includes pronghorn antelope, mule deer, javelina, mountain lions, an assortment of small mammals, amphibians and snakes, and neotropical migratory birds. The area is primitive with no facilities; sites are accessible only via rugged and unmarked roads (four-wheel drive recommended), although there is a short, easy hike to the Agua Fria River from the Badger Springs trailhead. Located 40 miles north of Phoenix via I-17; take the Badger Springs exit east: 623-580-5500.

Greg Gnesios   SPIDER ROCK AT CANYON DE CHELLY

CANYON DE CHELLY

Beneath thousand-foot-high sheer cliffs are hundreds of pictographs and ruins of Indian villages constructed between 350 and 1300 A.D. Antelope House and Mummy Cave in Canyon del Muerto (Canyon of the Dead) and White House in Canyon de Chelly (d'SHAY) are some of the most awesome cliff dwellings in the West. Visitors at the 800-foot-high Spider Rock stand on an overlook, 200 feet above the sandstone spire. Far below, the Rio de Chelly flows through the canyon. Traditional Navajo women clothed in red and purple tend their farms. Indian guides conduct tours in ex-military trucks and jeeps. Park rangers lead groups along the ruin trails.

The villages at Canyon de Chelly were inhabited by the Anasazi who were driven away possibly by droughts around 1350 A.D. Designated in 1931, Canyon de Chelly is located in northeastern Arizona, near Chinle. A visitor center near the entrance has displays explaining the history of the canyon and its inhabitants. The Monument is on the Navajo Reservation, where the Indians may demonstrate silver-smithing and other crafts. Travel in the canyons is allowed only with a ranger or an authorized guide, except the trail to White House Ruin. There are two spectacular Rim Drives, each about 35 miles round trip. The North has six scenic overlooks; the South eight. Chinle, AZ: 928-674-5500.

National Park Service   CASA GRANDE RUINS

Casa Grande Ruins & Hohokam Pima

It has been said that Casa Grande conjures up the image of Stonehenge, the primitive British astronomical observatory where ancients timed the planting of their crops. The presence of seven small holes in the top chamber, aimed toward the sky, seems to support this theory. But no one knows for certain if the four-story building was an observatory, fortress, temple, or apartment house. Casa Grande ("big house" in Spanish) was structured from lime-rich caliche clay that was strip-mined and moistened, then poured into courses 25 inches high. Ponderosa pine beams were brought from forests 60 miles away. By dating growth rings in the beams, archaeologists determined that it was built around 1350 A.D. It was surrounded by a walled village of pit-homes, roofed over with mud and sticks, which could be reached only by ladders.

Casa Grande was most likely built by Hohokam people. The Hohokams (a Pima Indian word meaning "those who have gone") surveyed and excavated 600 miles of irrigation canals along the Gila and Salt Rivers and maintained a large city six miles from the nearest water supply. They survived on "bumper crops" of corn, squash, and beans raised in circular fields. Trading far and wide in turquoise, copper bells, abalone shells, pinyon seeds, cotton cloth and bird feathers, they crafted amazingly intricate jewelry and beautiful pottery. Then around 1450 they disappeared. In 1892, this mass of structures was designated a national monument, as was the nearby Hohokam Pima National Monument. One mile north of Coolidge on Arizona Hwy. 87: 520-723-3172.

Chiricahua National Monument   ECHO CANYON

CHIRICAHUA

Called "Land of the Standing-Up Rocks" by the Chiricahua Apaches and "Wonderland of Rocks" by pioneers, this National Monument is high in the Chiricahua Mountains of southeast Arizona. The bizarre assembly of rock was formed 25 million years ago by violent volcanic explosions. Colored ash cooled and fused into an almost 2,000-foot thick layer of dark volcanic rock. A combination of water, wind, silt, ice, and sand took the next steps: sculpting and lifting the layers into contorted mountains and 200-foot spires. Multitudes of single rocks weighing hundreds of tons balance on tiny pedestals.

Led by Cochise and Geronimo, Chiricahua Apache Indians retreated across the valley to the Dragoon Mountains after raids. Because the region looked so haunted, it wasn't explored by white men until 1888, when Hughs Stafford and Niel Erikson entered in pursuit of Massai (Big Foot), an Apache who had stolen one of their horses. Chiricahua was named a national monument in 1924. A six-mile paved road and more than 17 miles of trails wind through the Monument, which is nearly surrounded by Coronado National Forest. Visitors can see the Heart of Rocks, Punch and Judy, Duck on a Rock, Totem Pole, and Big Balanced Rock, to name a few. A rock grotto, created by wind and water erosion, is the enchantment of Echo Canyon. Other surprises include a small natural bridge, and a ledge of volcanic hailstones. A visitor center features exhibits of the area's history and geography. Near Willcox: 520-824-3560.

Bette Ariel   PARASHANT

GRAND CANYON-PARASHANT

Deep canyons, mountains and solitary buttes illustrate the rich 2-billion-year geological history of the Colorado Plateau at this monument where Paleozoic and Mesozoic sedimentary rock layers remain largely intact and unobscured by vegetation. Designated in 2000—and called a scientific treasure because it comprises 1,054,264 acres of remote, unspoiled lands—Grand Canyon-Parashant is similar to Grand Canyon National Park, where canyon walls rise to a forested plateau. The lower Shivwits Plateau is a key watershed for the Colorado River and the Grand Canyon. Elevations at the monument range from 2,300 to 8,000 feet above sea level.

The area comprises a large number of fossils. Bryozoans and brachiopods can be found in the limestone of the Grand Wash Cliffs; brachiopods, pelecypods, fenestrate bryozoa and crinoid fossils are abundant in the Whitmore Canyon. Parashant Canyon contains sponges in nodules and pectenoid pelecypods. Flora and fauna include giant Mojave yucca, Joshua trees, penstemons, trophy deer, Kaibab squirrels, wild turkey, spotted bats and goshawk. Wildlife viewers can also see numerous threatened or endangered species such as the California condor, the Mexican spotted owl and the desert tortoise. Meanwhile, evidence of human existence over the centuries is apparent via village ruins, burial sites, rock art, historic ranch structures and mining sites. Managed jointly by the BLM and the National Park Service, the monument is located on the Colorado Plateau in northwestern Arizona. It borders Grand Canyon National Park to the south and the state of Nevada to the west; it also includes a portion of the Lake Mead National Recreation Area: 435-688-3200.

Courtesy BLM   IRONWOOD FOREST

IRONWOOD FOREST

The ironwood tree has long been considered a symbol of desert abundance. This hardy evergreen with iron-like wood grows 45 feet tall and can live up to 1,500 years. In the spring it sports pink or lavender flowers and bears seed pods relished by birds, small mammals and native people. This "nurse tree" shelters saguaro, night-blooming cereus and other plants from both cold and blistering sun as well as providing roosts for birds, burrows for tortoises, forage for desert bighorn sheep and nectar for bees.

Ironwood Forest National Monument—on 135,000 acres—is home to one of the most impressive stands of ironwood trees in the Sonoran Desert as well as to a wide diversity of plant, animal and bird life. Threatened and endangered species live here including the Nichols Turk's head cactus and lesser long-nosed bat. A breathtaking display of wildflowers lights up the area in spring. The monument borders the Tohono O`odham Tribal Lands, and encompasses the Silver Bell, Waterman, and Sawtooth mountain ranges, intersected by desert valleys, with elevation ranging from 1,800 to 4,261 feet. The monument also includes more than 200 Hohokam sites dating back to 600 A.D. and the ruins of a Spanish Mission constructed by the same priest who built San Xavier. Los Robles, Cocoraque Butte and Santa Ana del Chiquiburitac archeological districts are on the National Register of Historic Places. This monument, established in 2000, is managed by the Bureau of Land Management. There are no facilities; sites are accessible only via trails and rugged roads. Located 25 miles northwest of Tucson off I-10: 520-258-7200.

Arizona Office of Tourism   MONTEZUMA CASTLE

MONTEZUMA CASTLE & TUZIGOOT

One of the best-preserved cliff dwellings in the nation is the five-story, 20-room Montezuma Castle. Named by early settlers, who mistook it for an Aztec Indian building, it was constructed by Sinagua farmers around 1100. The hand-filled stone walls and foot-thick sycamore ceiling beams are 90 percent intact as the Indians fashioned them. A few miles north is Montezuma Well, a limestone sink formed long ago by the collapse of an underground cavern. Hohokam Indians who settled in the Verde Valley about 500 years before the Sinaguas, used the well for irrigation, as did the Sinaguas. They hunted, gathered, and mined salt from a nearby deposit. The pithouse (an underground house covered above-ground with poles and mud) at the Well was built by Hohokams around 1100. The one-room houses and 55-room pueblos were Sinaguan dwellings, occupied between 1125 and 1400.

Another Sinaguan village northwest of Montezuma comprises the site of Tuzigoot (Apache for "crooked water"). Perching atop a 120-foot ridge, it began in 1125 as a small cluster of rooms, expanding to more than 70 before the early 1400s when the Indians left the valley. Montezuma was designated a national monument in 1906 and Tuzigoot in 1939. Both monuments are located south of Flagstaff. Montezuma: 928-567-3322. Tuzigoot: 928-634-5564.

Bob Bradshaw   BETATAKIN RUIN

NAVAJO

This monument, called "Navajo" because of its location in the heart of the Navajo Reservation, was actually established in 1909 to protect three Anasazi cliff dwellings which dated back nearly 700 years. The Anasazis made use of cliff overhangs for their homes, adding on rooms as the population grew. Being deeply religious, they also built kivas—ceremonial chambers similar to the early pithouses. They traded corn, beans, and squash for cotton and turquoise. With a need for storage vessels, they soon developed pottery which often incorporated intricate, geometric designs.

Three distinct groups of Anasazi were present in the southwest in the 1200s. The Chaco group settled in New Mexico; the Mesa Verde division made its home in Colorado; and the Kayenta Anasazis moved into Arizona, into Tsegi Canyon, now the site of Navajo National Monument. Of the three dwellings at Navajo, Betatakin ("ledge house" in Navajo) was occupied from 1250 to 1300. It was a deep south-facing cave, which eventually may have held 125 persons who came to the village in groups. Tree-ring dating shows that early villagers cut and stockpiled many timbers for construction use by late-comers. Anasazis came to Keet Seel (Navajo for "broken pieces of pottery") much earlier, in 950. Stones and timbers from the earliest houses were reused for construction of the final village in 1250.

Kevin McKibbin   KEET SEEL RUIN

Apparently inhabitants regularly moved in and out of Keet Seel. A new surge of building around 1272, along with new styles of pottery, indicated a new group of people. More rooms were built nearby, possibly holding 150 toward the end. As families moved out, some abandoned rooms were converted into granaries. When the final tenants left, sealed doors suggest an intention to return. The third ruin, Inscription House, was built at about the same time as the others, but is smaller. T-shaped doorways and partial adobe construction distinguish it from Betatakin and Keet Seel.

Keet Seel was first discovered in 1895 by Richard Wetherill Betatakin and Inscription House in 1909 by John Wetherill. Because of its exposure to weather and its general fragility, it was closed to the public in 1968. Park headquarters are 60 miles northeast of Tuba City on U.S. 160. The half-mile Sandal Trail leads to an overlook with a view across the canyon of Betatakin Ruin. This strenuous, four-hour round trip hike, equivalent to walking up a 70-story building, can be visited only by guided tour. The trip to Keet Seel (summer only) is eight miles one way.

The Navajos, relative newcomers to Arizona, migrated from northern Canada in the 1400s. The acquisition of horses and sheep from the Spanish a century later made them a powerful nation. Today Navajoland covers more than 25,000 square miles in three states. Just to the north is Monument Valley, with amazing rock formations like the Left and Right Mitten, Totem Pole, and Sun's Eye. Near Tonlea: 928-672-2700.

D. Sokell   ORGAN PIPE CACTUS

ORGAN PIPE CACTUS

This monument was established in 1937 to protect the Organ Pipe and 30 other cacti species, 283 species of birds, and an abundance of reptiles, mammals, and insects, some found nowhere else in the U.S. This rare cactus forms a cluster of water-storing trunks resembling huge organ pipes 12 to 15 feet tall. (Annual rainfall here is 9-1/2 inches.) The Organ Pipe is limited in Arizona to a 500-square-mile region of the Sonoran Desert. The monument is also the only place in the U.S. to see the even more rare Senita cactus. Senita look similar to Organ Pipes but with gray whisker-like spines at the tops of the columns.

A visitor center features a slide presentation titled "Where Edges Meet: A Sonoran Sanctuary." The 21-mile Ajo Mountain Drive takes travelers into the Ajo Mountain Range and affords a spectacular view of a natural stone arch 35 feet high and 90 feet wide. Quitobaquito Springs, a veritable oasis on the route, is a bird-watcher's paradise. The 53-mile Puerto Blanco Drive circles the Puerto Blanco Mountains and touches the Mexican border.

The Tohono O'odham (Desert People) Indians, who have lived for centuries in the Sand Desert, harvest and eat the fleshy Organ Pipe cactus fruit. This tribe produces more baskets than any other in the U.S. Near Ajo: 520-387-5836

PIPE SPRING NATIONAL MONUMENT

PIPE SPRING

Pipe Spring was the only dependable water for 60 miles when Mormon missionaries camped here in 1858, but oddly enough, its namesake is a smoking pipe. In a shooting contest the missionaries held, one excellent marksman shot the bottom out of a pipe bowl. Five years later, James M. Whitmore built a dugout and brought sheep and cattle to the area. He and his sheepherder were massacred on January 6, 1866, by Navajos while pursuing members of the tribe who had stolen his sheep. After seven years of abandonment, Brigham Young established a fort for a church-operated cattle and dairy enterprise. It was constructed of squared red Chilean sandstone, with gunports and sturdy gates in case of attack. The building was in operation by 1871, serving as a ranch house, creamery, and as Arizona's first telegraph station until 1923, when it was declared a national monument.

Today people are attracted by Pipe Spring's living history and interpretive activities. In the spring, modern cowboys brand cattle from local ranches. Visitors are invited to assist in cookie and candy making, candle dipping and making rugs. A museum offers rooms full of antiques. Nineteenth-century bunkhouses, work sheds, and corrals are also open to the public. For nature-lovers, the Spring is an oasis for plants and wildlife. Numerous species of birds, small rodents, rabbits and coyotes have been spotted. Pipe Spring is remote: 15 miles southwest of Fredonia on Arizona Hwy. 389, near the Utah border. Near Moccasin: 928-643-7105.

Courtesy BLM   SONORAN DESERT

SONORAN DESERT

This monument, designated in 2000, celebrates the great Sonoran Desert—the most biologically diverse of the North American deserts. Your first impression will likely be of vast saguaro cactus forest communities, scattered throughout the 496,337 acres alongside palo verde trees, ironwood, prickly pear and cholla. You will also see three mountain ranges—the Maricopa, Sand Tank and Table Top Mountains—separated by wide valleys, and involving three wilderness areas. Scanning the desert landscape, it's hard to believe that 20,000 years ago this arid region was once a lush juniper-oak-pinion pine woodland that received abundant precipitation. Today, with scant rain, inhabitants of the desert rely heavily on tiaras, water holes that occur throughout the monument. An abundance of wildlife makes this area its home, including mule deer, javelina, mountain lion, gray fox, bobcat, and a large population of desert bighorn sheep. You can also see more than 200 species of birds, the endangered lesser long-nosed bat, and a variety of reptiles and amphibians, such as the red-backed whiptail and the Sonoran desert tortoise, which range over 25,000 acres in the Maricopa Mountains.

The area is believed to have been a crucial travel route between the Hohokam and tribes living in what is now Mexico. Indeed, you can view signs of large prehistoric villages with rock art, lithic quarries, and various artifacts. Here, too, are many important historic trails, including the Juan Bautista de Anza National Historic Trail; eventually this trail will be 600 miles long, and will be the first International Historic Trail in the world. The monument is primitive, with no facilities, and has only unpaved roads. Located in south central Arizona, 60 miles from Phoenix: 602-417-9300.

Greg Gnesios   SUNSET CRATER

SUNSET CRATER & WUPATKI

Over 900 years ago, Sunset Crater was an active volcanic cinder cone, formed by an eruption. Molten rock exploded from a crack in the ground (causing a vent), rose high into the air, solidified quickly, and fell back to earth. Subsequent eruptions over a period of 200 years accumulated debris around the vent, creating a 1,000-foot cone. The final outburst of lava contained iron and sulphur which oxidized into red and yellow particles. These fiery particles settled on the rim of the cone, giving it a magnificent, sunset-like glow. A similar set of smaller eruptions created the sculpture garden at the Crater's base. Smaller cones formed and moving lava cooled to a crust on the earth. Heated material beneath the surface then drained away, creating caves. One such cave has ice over it much of the year, the result of a dead-end tube, from which lava drained. Sunset Crater is just the "baby" in the area; volcanoes in the San Francisco volcanic field had been erupting for several million years prior to Sunset's creation. This field, including Sunset Crater, makes up 2,000 square miles of the southwestern Colorado Plateau.

Two lava flows destroyed all living things in their paths, carrying debris for many miles. To the northeast, lava and cinders buried the villages of the Sinagua Indians who had cultivated the dry rocky land for 400 years. Some of the Sinagua (meaning "without water") migrated to Wupatki along with Anasazi Indians from the northeast and Cohonina Indians from the west. A few decades after the eruptions, the tribes discovered the soil was more productive than before. Thin layers of ash on the earth absorbed

17

Shirley Hoh   SUNSET CRATER

moisture and heat and prevented evaporation, which leng-
thened the growing season. Scientists speculate that climatic changes resulted in more water. These three groups of
Indians shared construction and farming techniques,
advanced in their pottery forms, held religious ceremonies,
athletic contests, and intermarried. Between 1215 and 1225
A.D., they slowly disbanded and moved on, leaving only
migratory peoples to inhabit the area. Both the destruction
and removal of archaeological artifacts prompted
Wupatki's designation as a national monument in 1924.
Even so, in the 1930s, researchers doing tree-ring dating
discovered a whiskey still, its vats fired from timbers
removed from the pueblo ruins.

The ruins at Wupatki (Hopi for "tall house") are almost
camouflaged by the dry, parched land around them. Sinaguas
constructed free-standing stone pueblos, from small one-story
homes to multi-leveled buildings with more than 100 rooms.
Rounded stone courts were used for athletic competitions.
Ceremonials were held in a 50-foot-diameter amphitheater.
The Wupatki pueblos are open sunrise to sunset and so is
the visitor center. Both monuments are reached by entering
the Sunset Crater-Wupatki Loop off of U.S. Highway 89
north of Flagstaff. Sunset Crater: 928-526-0502. Wupatki:
928-679-2365.

Tonto National Monument   LOWER RUIN

TONTO

Tonto's superb collection of artifacts has enabled anthropologists to discern a great deal about its ancient inhabitants, the Salado Indians. Beads, shells, shards, and bones have helped assess the hunting-gathering-farming lifestyles of the Salados. Historians have identified more than 300 wild plants used for food, fiber, and medicines. The men were about 5-1/2 feet tall, women five feet even. All had small faces and delicate features, their heads slightly flattened in the back from being on cradleboards as infants. The Salados' teeth were ground down from grit in their food.

The Salados (meaning "salty" in Spanish) farmed the Salt River Valley from 1150 to 1450 A.D., aided by extensive irrigated canals. They lived first in crude masonry structures, then moved to the high natural caves of Tonto, where they constructed three villages of mud and stone. Some sections of the dwellings were two stories high and contained more than 40 rooms. Sandals, mats, baskets, headbands, cradleboards, cordage made from yucca plants, clothing, blankets, and tools have been discovered. Salado textiles were some of the finest, employing lace-like open weaves and diamond twills; they were dyed in an assortment of colors. Today a self-guided tour leads to the Lower Ruin. Guided tours are available for the Upper Ruin. A visitor center exhibits Salado artifacts. A national monument since 1907, Tonto is 29 miles northwest of Globe. A visit to Tonto National Monument should include the Apache Trail, a scenic 25-mile drive on Arizona Highway 88: 928-467-2241.

Chris Tincher   PARIA CANYON

VERMILION CLIFFS

Recognized as a "geological treasure," this 293,000-acre monument was designated in 2000. At its center is the Paria Plateau, a spectacular terrace stretched between two prominent geologic structures: the East Kaibab and Echo Cliffs monoclines. The 3,000-foot-high Vermilion Cliffs are to the south, resplendent in their multicolored layers of shale and sandstone. To the east is the 2,500-foot-deep Paria River Canyon, winding along the plateau to the Colorado River; sedimentary rocks eroded in the canyon have created amphitheaters, arches, massive stone walls and other geologic features. The Coyote Buttes in the northwest are a marvel unto themselves: Navajo Sandstone crossbeds banded in red, pink, orange and yellow—the result of manganese, iron and other oxides precipitating into the rock.

Vegetation in the area is comprised of both warm desert grassland and cold desert flora. Particularly notable is Welsh's milkweed, a threatened plant specific to Utah and Arizona, which colonizes and stabilizes shifting sand dunes but is easily overtaken by other encroaching plants. Desert bighorn sheep, pronghorn antelope and mountain lions are abundant here, along with 20 species of raptors including the endangered California condor.

Human existence on the plateau and surrounding canyons dates back more than 12,000 years. Some of the earliest rock art in the Southwest can be found in the monument as well as Ancestral Puebloan village ruins and settlements left behind by Spanish and Mormon explorers. One Mormon exploratory route gained fame as the Honeymoon Trail because Mormon couples seeking to have their marriages solemnized at the Mormon temple in St. George, Utah, traveled it. Current day travelers can access a moderate 6-mile day hike into Paria Canyon-Vermilion Cliffs Wilderness Area, which offers magnificent views of House Rock Valley. The monument is located west of Page in northern Arizona: 435-688-3200.

Russ Finley   ISLAND TRAIL—WALNUT CANYON

WALNUT CANYON

Sinaguas, whom archaeologists believe were the ancestors of some present-day Pueblo Indians, farmed Walnut Canyon around 800 A.D. Moving in from nearby sites, they first built brush-covered pithouses. Two hundred years later, the Sinaguas decided to live beneath cliff overhangs that lined the 400-foot-deep canyon. They partitioned ledges into houses, added a front wall with a door, and a smoke hole just under the top of the ledge. The canyon had a dependable supply of water and an abundance of plants and animals. Their ancestors for 50,000 years had hunted game, dressed in skins, and gathered fruit; and so did the Sinaguas. They also crafted black and white ceramics and extracted food, fibers, medicines, and fuel from ponderosa pine and other native plants. Walnut Canyon was the home of the Sinaguas for 3-1/2 centuries before they mysteriously vanished.

The canyon was unoccupied for 600 years before being rediscovered in 1883. The remains of more than 300 cliff dwellings are part of a national monument established in 1915. The 3/4-mile Rim Trail follows the canyon rim and rugged Island Trail actually leads into the dwellings via a 185-foot descent. A museum displays a history of the canyon. Walnut Canyon is 7-1/2 miles east of Flagstaff (exit 204) on I-40. 928-526-3367.

Greg Gnesios THE MISSION AT TUMACACORI

TUMACACORI

Tumacacori was designated a national monument in 1908 to commemorate the introduction of Spanish civilization into Arizona. Spanish influence began in 1691 with the arrival of the Jesuit missionary, Father Kino, who celebrated Mass from a brush shelter built for him by the Piman Indians. For 20 years he held services and encouraged ranching and farming. The mission was moved to its present site after the Pima Rebellion of 1751, and was named San Jose de Tumacacori. Jesuits were replaced by the Franciscan Order in 1768, and Tumacacori became headquarters for the chain of area missions.

By 1821, when Mexico won independence from Spain, all missions but Tumacacori had been abandoned. Without government aid, defense against frequent Apache raids was impossible. Devout Christian Indians moved church relics to San Xavier, outside Tucson, and the mission was abandoned in 1848.

The present church, built around 1800, features baroque architecture and an unfinished bell tower of burnt brick. A self-guided walk takes visitors to the church, a cemetery, and an unfinished mortuary chapel. A museum highlights early Indian and Spanish history. The monument is 43 miles south of Tucson on I-19: 520-398-2341.

Fort Bowie N.H.S.   APACHE CAMP—FORT BOWIE

FORT BOWIE

The postal service motto "…Despite rain, snow, sleet or hail…" could have been no more appropriately applied than to the Butterfield Overland Mail Route, in the Fort Bowie region. Replacing the original "Jackass Mail" system in 1858, it required passage over the dangerous Apache Pass, in the heart of Apache Land. The Chiricahua Apaches had settled the area some 200 years before, attracted by Apache Spring. Hunting, gathering, raiding neighboring villages, and protecting their territories using horses acquired from the Spanish, was their lifestyle. As the Anglo-American frontier moved westward in the mid-1800s, the Apaches were faced with sharing their territory. The Bascom Affair of the U.S. Army, a mission to rescue a kidnapped boy and stolen livestock, resulted in the 10 year Chiricahua Indian Wars. A year later, Fort Bowie was built nearby, to aid Union forces, and protect supply lines.

Ten years after the fort was built, peace was made, and 3,000 square miles in southeastern Arizona were established as an Apache Reservation. Many Indians were dissatisfied with this settlement. Small bands led by Geronimo and others instituted new raids. In 1886 the Southwest Indian Wars finally ended, and in 1894, Fort Bowie was abandoned for lack of need. The site was authorized in 1964 to preserve the Apache Pass Stage Station, Apache Spring, the Fort Bowie Complex, and a portion of the Butterfield Overland Mail Route. There is no road to the actual ruins, which are accessible via a 3-mile-round-trip walking trail. Fort Bowie is located south of Willcox off Arizona Highway 186: 520-847-2500.

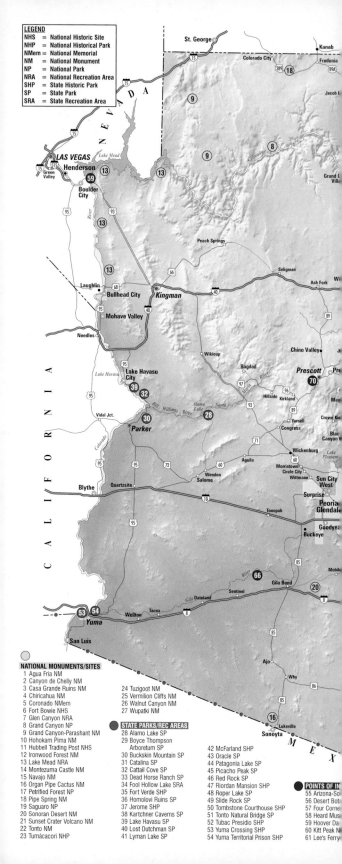

NATIONAL MONUMENTS/SITES

1 Agua Fria NM
2 Canyon de Chelly NM
3 Casa Grande Ruins NM
4 Chiricahua NM
5 Coronado NMem
6 Fort Bowie NHS
7 Glen Canyon NRA
8 Grand Canyon NP
9 Grand Canyon-Parashant NM
10 Hohokam Pima NM
11 Hubbell Trading Post NHS
12 Ironwood Forest NM
13 Lake Mead NRA
14 Montezuma Castle NM
15 Navajo NM
16 Organ Pipe Cactus NM
17 Petrified Forest NP
18 Pipe Spring NM
19 Saguaro NP
20 Sonoran Desert NM
21 Sunset Crater Volcano NM
22 Tonto NM
23 Tumácacori NHP
24 Tuzigoot NM
25 Vermilion Cliffs NM
26 Walnut Canyon NM
27 Wupatki NM

STATE PARKS/REC AREAS

28 Alamo Lake SP
29 Boyce Thompson Arboretum SP
30 Buckskin Mountain SP
31 Catalina SP
32 Cattail Cove SP
33 Dead Horse Ranch SP
34 Fool Hollow Lake SRA
35 Fort Verde SHP
36 Homolovi Ruins SP
37 Jerome SHP
38 Kartchner Caverns SP
39 Lake Havasu SP
40 Lost Dutchman SP
41 Lyman Lake SP
42 McFarland SHP
43 Oracle SP
44 Patagonia Lake SP
45 Picacho Peak SP
46 Red Rock SP
47 Riordan Mansion SHP
48 Roper Lake SP
49 Slide Rock SP
50 Tombstone Courthouse SHP
51 Tonto Natural Bridge SP
52 Tubac Presidio SP
53 Yuma Crossing SHP
54 Yuma Territorial Prison SHP

POINTS OF IN

55 Arizona-So
56 Desert Bot
57 Four Corne
58 Heard Mus
59 Hoover Da
60 Kitt Peak N
61 Lee's Ferry

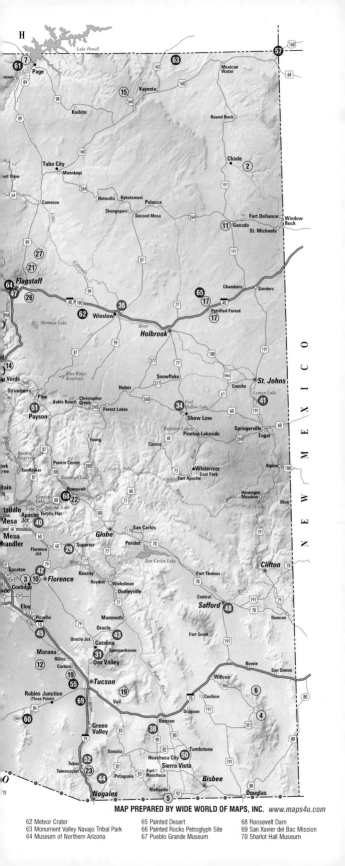

62 Meteor Crater
63 Monument Valley Navajo Tribal Park
64 Museum of Northern Arizona

65 Painted Desert
66 Painted Rocks Petroglyph Site
67 Pueblo Grande Museum

68 Roosevelt Dam
69 San Xavier del Bac Mission
70 Sharlot Hall Museum

HUBBELL TRADING POST

HUBBELL TRADING POST

Designated a national historic site in 1965, Hubbell Trading Post remains the bartering center that it was in the 1870s, the oldest continually operating trading post on the Navajo Indian Reservation. Its founder was John Lorenzo Hubbell, an early organizer of Arizona statehood. Hubbell saw himself on a mission to help Navajos better understand whites. Setting up the post (and later 24 others), he sold Navajo products, counseled the Indians, and supplied medical aid. During the smallpox epidemic of 1886, he turned his house into an infirmary. The Indians, who had seen Hubbell as a friend and equal until then, now venerated him as magical because he didn't catch the illness himself (he had had it as a child and was immune). When Hubbell died in 1930, he was mourned by the Navajo population. He is buried on a hill behind his house, overlooking the trading post. His wife and his closest Navajo friend, Many Horses, are buried beside him.

Navajos, Zunis, Hopis, and other tribes still sell and trade handwoven rugs, jewelry, baskets, and pottery here. A nearby visitor center offers weaving and silversmithing demonstrations and collections of artifacts and art. Guided tours are available of Hubbell's museum-like home. The walls are lined with western art, ceilings adorned with Indian baskets, and beautiful Navajo rugs cover the floors. Hubbell Trading Post, one mile west of Ganado, is operated through the National Park Service. 928-755-3475

Coronado National Memorial   VISITOR CENTER

CORONADO

Coronado National Memorial commemorates Hispanic heritage and the first major exploration of the American Southwest by Europeans. Officially established in 1952, its namesake is Francisco Vasquez de Coronado, the Spanish explorer who marched through Arizona in 1540. From spectacular Montezuma Pass, a three-mile scenic drive above the Memorial, it is easy to spy on the past. Imagine Coronado with his 336 uniformed Spanish soldiers, four priests, several hundred Mexican-Indian allies, and 1,500 animals. The entourage left Mexico in search of the fabled "Cities of Cibola." Rumors promised that these cities were large, lined with goldsmith shops, and houses of many stories, with emerald and turquoise studded doorways. No such fortune met Coronado. Instead he encountered hostile Indians in stone pueblos, and the richness of the land that is the Southwest. He returned, deeming the expedition a failure, not realizing how he had paved the way for further Spanish exploration and colonization.

Set in oak woodlands on the Mexican border at the southern end of the Huachuca Mountains, the land is a celebration in itself. Views from Montezuma Pass take in the San Rafael Valley to the Patagonia and Santa Rita Mountains. Baboquivari Peak on the Papago Indian Reservation can be seen on a clear day. Schott's Yucca, used by Indians for food and cord-making, grows along with cane chollas for making canes. Birds, coati, peccary, white-tailed deer, bobcats, and (rarely) mountain lions, have been sighted here. Near Hereford: 520-366-5515

Arizona Office of Tourism   GRAND CANYON

GRAND CANYON

One of the most spectacular natural wonders of the world, the Grand Canyon is one mile deep, 600 feet to 18 miles wide, and 277 miles long. It was formed 1,700 million years ago when large mountains pushed upward, eroded, and were replaced by a huge basin created by volcanic rumblings in the earth. Sediments and rocks collected in the basin; 900 million years later these layers formed another mountain range, which also eroded. By 225 million years ago the basin was edged with layered sandstones, shale, and limestone; this comprised the upper three-quarters of the Grand Canyon's walls. Approximately 160 million years after that the whole region rose above sea level. Moisture falling on the newly formed Rocky Mountains created the Colorado River. The river easily carried boulders; this power of water, earth and rock (in conjunction with wind, ice and heat) carved the current Grand Canyon.

Nearly 2,500 archaeological sites show that people inhabited the canyon dating back 4,000 years. Small, split-twig figurines discovered in the Redwall Limestone caves are believed to be objects of hunting magic used around 2500 B.C. About 1,000 years ago the Anasazi (ancestors of the Hopis) farmed the region, constructed stone and mud buildings, and left stone tools and pottery. Migratory groups and explorers appeared after the Anasazi left. John Wesley Powell (namesake of Lake Powell) mined the canyon in the late 1800s. Today Grand Canyon National Park comprises

Arizona Department of Tourism   MULE TRAIL

nearly 1.22 million acres and has a range of scenic areas and activities, attracting 3 million visitors annually.

The Grand Canyon is divided into two sections: the North Rim and the South Rim. The North Rim is largely a spruce-fir forest 1,000 feet higher in altitude than the South Rim. Due to this elevation and its greater snowfall the North Rim is only open from mid-May to late October. The dryer South Rim is open year-round and has a wide range of facilities. The 20.8-mile Kaibab Trail wanders from one Rim to the other, crossing the Colorado River on a suspension bridge wide enough to hold one person and a mule. It winds through Phantom Ranch, where meals and accommodations are available with reservations.

The South Rim visitor center has a small museum and bookstore. The nearby Yavapai Museum has a panorama of the Canyon and geological exhibits. A paved 3-1/4-mile nature trail extends along the rim. Desert View is 23 miles to the east, overlooking the Painted Desert and the Colorado River. The Tusayan Museum offers human history exhibits; a self-guided trail leads to Anasazi ruins. The main North Rim information station is located in Grand Canyon Lodge at Bright Angel Point. Transept Canyon offers a 1-1/2 mile walk along the North Rim, and the North Kaibab Trail stretches nine miles down to the inner canyon. Another way to tour the area is by mule. Groups of mules (called mule strings) have made daily trips up and down the Canyon since the early 1900s. River rafting and scenic air tours are also popular methods of viewing the area. For more information call 928-638-7888.

Arizona Office of Tourism   PETRIFIED FOREST

PETRIFIED FOREST &
THE PAINTED DESERT

The giant rainbow-colored stone logs are reminiscent of a magical fallen forest, with bits of Painted Desert and pre-historic petroglyphs (paintings) strewn in between. Add numerous ancient ruins of Indian dwellings built with the stone, and you have the world's greatest concentration of petrified wood. About 225 million years ago this area of northeastern Arizona was interwoven with streams which comprised a vast flood plain. Large pine-like trees grew near the streams' headwaters. When the trees fell, they were swirled along with mud, sand, and volcanic ash into the flooding waters and became buried. Lack of oxygen prevented normal decay. Chemicals in the streams eventually dissolved mineral silica, which was absorbed into the logs' cells and holes. As water evaporated, only silica remained inside the logs, finally turning them to quartz. Surrounding deposits hardened into sandstones and shales of the Chinle Formation.

The area was left untouched, except by Indians who built villages with petrified logs and sandstone more than 600 years ago. The ruins, along with petroglyphs, can still be seen. The Petrified Forest was recorded by explorers in the mid-1800s. Unthinking people picked up the precious gemstones and logs until it seemed there would be none left. For protection, the area was established as a national monument

30

Petrified Forest   PAINTED DESERT OVERLOOK

in 1906. In 1962, the Petrified Forest became a national park. Today it includes more than 93,532 acres.

The Painted Desert is aptly named, a mixture of colors and shapes accented by badlands (barren land with eroded ridges, peaks, and mesas) and thousands of brilliant petrified logs. Small peaks resembling teepees or haystacks, demonstrate erosion of soft, layered clay deposits "painted" with carbon and iron oxide. A 27-mile-long paved road connects two visitor centers, and branches off for guided walks and scenic overlooks. The Painted Desert Visitor Center (near I-40) features a movie about the area's geological history. The Rainbow Forest Museum (near U.S. 180) displays polished petrified wood, fossils, and minerals, and offers diagrams explaining how badlands and petrified logs are formed. Outstanding specimens of petrified wood are on the short paved trail behind the museum.

Hundreds of skeletons of dinosaurs, phytosaurs, and other related creatures have been unearthed in Petrified Forest National Park. Phytosaurs were large crocodile-like reptiles, thought to precede dinosaurs. They were abundant and especially ferocious. Paleontologists speculate that many reptiles and amphibians in this era evolved armored scales as protection from phytosaurs. In 1985, one of the world's oldest dinosaur skeletons was discovered in the Petrified Forest. Affectionately nicknamed "Gertie," this small dinosaur dates back 225 million years to the first dinosaurs. Gertie probably lived in the shade of the giant trees, which later became petrified. Petrified Forest National Park: 928-524-6228.

Courtesy NPS   SAGUARO

SAGUARO

The Saguaro cactus is the symbol of the American southwest, and is the largest cactus in the United States. A Saguaro (sah-WAH-row) can grow up to 50 feet tall, weigh 10 tons, and have a possible life span of 200 years. Its stem and branches actually store water, enabling it to survive in this arid climate. The white, funnel-shaped blossoms that appear at night in May and June, are Arizona's state flower. Saguaro National Monument was established outside Tucson in 1933 to protect this important plant. In 1994 it was designated a national park.

Saguaro forests cover thousands of acres. As numerous as they seem to be in southern and western Arizona, it is estimated that only one of every 275,000 pinhead-sized seeds reaches maturity. Mature plants quickly create full "communities." The red, fleshy fruit is relished by wildlife and harvested by Indians. In the fleshy stems, gila woodpeckers and flickers drill holes for nesting sites. These sites are later used as homes by other birds.

The park spreads over nearly 90,000 acres in two Districts. The large Rincon Mountain area offers hiking trails, scenic overlooks, and stands of old Saguaros. The Tucson Mountain District is smaller but is the site of dense stands of Saguaros. Numerous other forms of plant and animal life can be studied at Saguaro National Park. Each district has a visitor center with exhibits and daily naturalist programs. 520-733-5153.

Arizona Office of Tourism SAILING ON LAKE POWELL

GLEN CANYON

About 60 million years ago, the rapid Colorado River carved deep canyons and dramatic fjord-like coves from sedimentary rock, creating Glen Canyon. Between 1956 and 1964, the Bureau of Reclamation stopped the river with Glen Canyon Dam and backed it up into these canyons. The water that gushed into the nooks and crannies became known as Lake Powell—186 miles long, with close to 2,000 miles of shoreline and more than 96 side canyons. Lake Powell and its surrounding rose-colored cliffs, mountains, and canyons comprise 1.25 million acres of Northern Arizona and Southern Utah—the Glen Canyon National Recreation Area.

Anasazi Indians (whose name in Navajo means "Ancient Ones") lived along these canyon bottoms in pre-lake days, beginning 2,000 years ago. They hunted and farmed, built pueblos, and left behind tools of stone and bone, pottery, and baskets. When droughts threatened the area in 1200 A.D., the Indians moved on, as did many Arizona people of that era. Subsequent migratory groups and Anglo and Spanish explorers passed through, but did not settle. In 1869 and in 1871–72, John Wesley Powell explored the area extensively. He called it Glen Canyon because of the many wooded "glens" along the banks of the Colorado River and up the side canyons. Today Lake Powell is punctuated with colorful sailing craft, large houseboats, and

Glen Canyon N.R.A.   LOOKING ACROSS WAHWEAP BAY

water skiers behind power boats. Canoes and kayaks navigate the narrow side canyons where the Indians lived, becoming cast in shadows that crawl down the walls. A long cruise up-water and a short jaunt up Forbidding and Bridge Canyons treat explorers to Rainbow Bridge (actually in Utah), the largest known natural stone bridge and one of the seven natural wonders of the world.

Warm, sandy beaches at Wahweap and all along the shore are attractive to swimmers. Wahweap, near Page, also has lodging, food service, a campground, boat rentals, and lake tours. Fishermen delight in bass, rainbow trout, striped bass, and crappie, with the cold clear water below the dam at Lee's Ferry being particularly popular for trout. Lee's Ferry is a historic crossing point on the river. A pioneer fort, post office, ranch buildings and relics remain from the area's past.

Hiking is another way to see Glen Canyon. Rich plant and animal life can be examined up close: lichen-streaked rocks, cacti and wildflowers, lizards, the tracks of coyotes, foxes, or deer. Indian ruins remain throughout the canyons. Camping is permitted in designated campgrounds and along the shore, from or on a boat. Glen Canyon is most accessible from its southern portion at Page on U.S. 89. A visitor center is located there and scenic flights are available from the Page Airport. Glen Canyon Dam is used for water storage and to produce hydroelectric power used throughout the West. Near Page: 928-608-6200.

Lake Mead. N.R.A   LAKE MEAD

LAKE MEAD

Established in 1936 as the country's first national recreation area, Lake Mead is one of man's most marvelous magic acts. Originally a desert region, the lake was created when the 726-foot high Hoover Dam tamed the wild Colorado River. The dam took 5,000 men five years to complete and was declared "an engineering victory" by President Franklin D. Roosevelt. A few years later Davis Dam was built downstream to create Lake Mohave. Today the Recreation Area encompasses almost 1.5 million acres of northwestern Arizona and southern Nevada with a wealth of terrains: desert, mountains, canyons, and primitive backcountry.

Nine developed areas with campgrounds are accessible by car or boat. Lake Mead and Lake Mohave offer more than 180 miles of aquatic pleasure. Both lakes have swimming beaches; marinas rent fishing boats, ski boats, waterskiing equipment and houseboats. Boat tours and raft trips run to Hoover Dam, the narrow, steep-walled gorge of Iceberg Canyon, and Lake Mohave's impressive Black Canyon. The lakes are also good sighting points for a variety of birds and wildlife including Desert Bighorn sheep.

Lakeshore and Northshore trips along Lake Mead highlight panoramic views of the lake against the dramatic desert mountains. Redstone Picnic Area sports colorful sandstone formations, and the road to Pearce Ferry crosses a spectacular Joshua-tree forest. Unpaved roads access the backcountry, the Shivwits Plateau and petroglyph sites. The main access to the Recreation Area is via U.S. 93 from Las Vegas, Nevada to Kingman, Arizona: 928-754-3030.

Arizona Office of Tourism   SAN FRANCISCO PEAKS

NATIONAL FORESTS

The Southwestern Region of the Forest Service, a division of the U.S. Department of Agriculture, administers six National Forests in Arizona. Each National Forest is directed by a Forest Supervisor and three to eight District Forest Rangers. A variety of recreational opportunities are available on both developed and undeveloped sites in National Forests. Fees are charged for many recreational sites and campgrounds; toilet facilities, family camp units, and water are available in those areas.

The Southwestern Region of the Forest Service, a division of the U.S. Department of Agriculture, administers the six Arizona forests found on page 37. The three Natural Conservation Areas on page 38, as well as the Wilderness Areas and one Primitive Area, are all located within the boundaries of the forests while administered by the Bureau of Land Management.

The mission of the Forest Service is to preserve a part of our national heritage in its natural state. A variety of recreational opportunities are available on both developed and undeveloped sites in National Forests. Fees are charged for many recreational sites and campgrounds; toilet facilities, family camp units, and water are usually available in those areas. Trails can be traversed on foot, bicycle, skis, horseback or burro. Laws prohibit removal of property and plants and protect archaeological sites. For maps, permits and reservations, visit www.fs.fed.us for the Forest Service and www.blm.gov for the Bureau of Land Management.

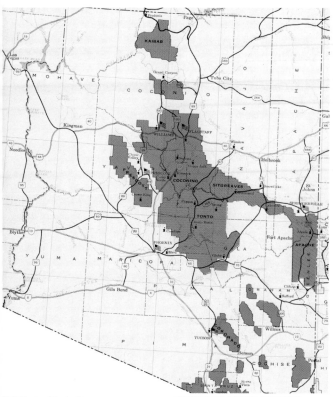

U.S. Dept. of Agriculture   ARIZONA NATIONAL FORESTS

NATIONAL FORESTS

Apache-Sitgraves   **Headquarters: Springerville**
Located in the rim country made famous by Zane Grey, the forest
surrounds 34 lakes and the headwaters of Arizona rivers.

Coconino   **Headquarters: Flagstaff**
A pine-covered plateau cut by deep canyons and bordered on the
south by the spectacular Mogollon Rim.

Coronado   **Headquarters: Tucson**
Spans across southeastern Arizona with spectacular views from
12 widely scattered mountain ranges that rise dramatically from
the desert floor.

Kaibab   **Headquarters: Williams**
Part of the United State's largest contiguous ponderosa pine forest,
Kaibab borders both the north and south rims of the Grand Canyon.

Prescott   **Headquarters: Prescott**
Here you will find year-round opportunities for camping, fishing,
hiking, horseback riding, photography, and picnicking.

Tonto   **Headquarters: Phoenix**
Scenic landscapes range from cactus-studded desert to pine forested
mountains along with abundant opportunity for recreation.

CONSERVATION AREAS

Gila Box Riparian National Conservation Area—Near Safford, includes portions of the Gila and San Francisco Rivers. Attractions include wildlife and river floating.

Las Cienegas National Conservation Area—50 miles southeast of Tucson, desert grasslands and oak-studded hills protect a diverse assemblage of plants and animals.

San Pedro Riparian National Conservation Area
Near Sierra Vista and anchored by 40 miles of the San Pedro River, there are numerous wildlife and recreation opportunities.

WILDERNESS AREAS

Areas are followed by the name of the National Forest in which they are located. Use the website www.reserveusa.gov or call 877-444-6777 to make reservations.

APACHE CREEK (Prescott)
BEAR WALLOW (Apache-Sitgreaves)
CASTLE CREEK (Prescott)
CEDAR BENCH (Prescott)
CHIRICAHUA (Coronado)
ESCUDILLA (Apache-Sitgreaves)
FOSSIL SPRINGS (Coconino)
FOUR PEAKS (Tonto)
GALIURO (Coronado)
GRANITE MOUNTAIN (Prescott)
HELLSGATE (Tonto)
JUNIPER MESA (Prescott)
KACHINA PEAKS (Coconino)
KANAB CREEK (Kaibab)
KENDRICK MOUNTAIN (Coconino)
MAZATZAL (Tonto)
MILLER PEAK (Coronado)
MOUNT BALDY (Apache-Sitgreaves)
MOUNT WRIGHTSON (Coronado)
MUNDS MOUNTAIN (Coconino)
PAJARITA (Coronado)
PINE MOUNTAIN (Between Prescott and Tonto)
PUSCH RIDGE (Coronado)
RED ROCK-SECRET MOUNTAIN (Coconino)
RINCON MOUNTAIN (Coronado)
SADDLE MOUNTAIN (Kaibab)
SALOME (Tonto)
SALT RIVER CANYON (Tonto)
SANTA TERESA (Coronado)
SIERRA ANCHA (Tonto)
STRAWBERRY CRATER (Coconino)
SUPERSTITION (Tonto)
SYCAMORE CANYON (Prescott, Kaibab, Coconino)
WEST CLEAR CREEK (Coconino)
WET BEAVER (Coconino)
WOODCHUTE (Prescott)
BLUE RANGE PRIMITIVE AREA (Apache-Sitgreaves)

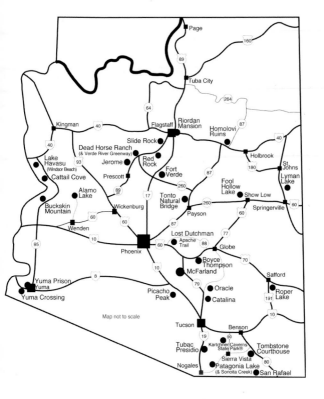

STATE PARKS

* S.P. = State Park; S.H.P. = State Historic Park; N.A. = Natural Area; R.A. = Recreation Area

Arizona has a wealth of state parks, many of which have camping, recreational facilities and trails leading to wilderness areas. Others offer interpretive information surrounding the site's history. Most have minimal entrance fees, although accompanied children ages 17 and under are admitted free. Handicap access is often available. For information: 602-542-4174 or www.pr.state.az.us.

Alamo Lake S.P.* is a fisherman's haven, particularly for bass, catfish, or bluegill. Water sports, picnicking, and camping are also popular. The area features a variety of desert plants and animals. (38 miles north of Wenden off U.S. Highway 60)

Boyce Thompson Arboretum S.P., sprawled on 420 acres of native and imported vegetation, features more than 1,277 different plant species. Two public greenhouses display cacti and succulents from deserts all over the world. Scenic nature trails weave through botanical gardens, set against the base of 4,400-foot Picket Post Mountain. The visitor center emphasizes local history and geology, exhibits plants used by Arizona Indians. (60 miles east of Phoenix on US Highway 60; 520-689-2811)

Buckskin Mountain S.P., tucked between scenic bluffs and the Colorado River, offers camping, picnicking, water sports, and hiking. (11 miles north of Parker on Arizona Highway 95)

Catalina S.P., at the base of the Catalina Mountains, offers 5,500 acres of varied plant and wildlife, picnicking, camping, and horseback riding. Hikers delight in trail access to the Coronado National Forest. (9 miles north of Tucson on Arizona Highway 77)

Dead Horse Ranch S.P. is a quiet place to camp, picnic, watch birds, fish, and meander through cottonwood groves along the Verde (Spanish for "green") River. (Across the river from Cottonwood, off 5th Street)

Fool Hollow Lake R.A., located at 6,300 feet in the Apache-Sitgreaves National Forest, is a scenic getaway for picnickers and fisherman alike. The recreation area is located 15 miles from The White Mountain Trail System – 103 miles of hiking on 11 loop trails. (north of Show Low off Highway 260)

Fort Verde S.H.P. was a major military base during Indian campaigns of the 1870s. An "Officers' Row" of home and history exhibits illustrate 19th century Arizona soldiering. (3 miles east of I-17 in Camp Verde)

Homolovi Ruins S.P. preserves a community of Anasazi people who lived here in the 1200s and 1300s during their migrations to the Hopi Mesas in the north. Today Homolovi is sacred to the Hopis, descendants of the Anasazi. The park features three main pueblo ruins, more than 300 archaeological sites, a visitor center, exhibits, and trails. (north of Winslow off Highway 87)

Jerome S.H.P. commemorates this once-flourishing copper mining community, labeled by an early New York newspaper "the wickedest town in the West." At the mining museum, former mansion of Arizona pioneer James D. Douglas ("Rawhide Jimmie") in the 1870s, visitors can hear stories of the people, places, and technology of Arizona's mining history. Panoramic views of Jerome and the Verde Valley. (Between Prescott and Flagstaff on US Highway 89A)

Kartchner Caverns S.P.—A recent visitor to Kartchner was heard to exclaim, "It's the Grand Canyon of state parks!" Indeed, this limestone cave with more than two miles of passages and two football field-sized rooms is grand, indeed. 330 million years ago this underground

Noelle Wilson KARTCHNER CAVERNS STATE PARK®

wonder began as an inland sea with sediment deposits that hardened into limestone. Then acidic rainwater etched passages into the stones and created a large and colorful variety of formations called "speleothems." Another major attraction of Kartchner is the group of more than 1,000 female bats who use the Big Room for a nursery in the summer and emerge en masse from the cave each evening until mid-September. The park also features a 23,000 square foot Discovery Center with exhibits (including a replica of the cave), regional and interactive displays and educational information. Visitors can access hiking trails and the Hummingbird Garden. (Near Benson, off State Hwy 90; 520-586-4100 for information, 520-586-CAVE (2283) for reservations.

Lake Havasu S.P. offers 45 lakeshore miles of resort living and boat-access camping. Outside the park in nearby Lake Havasu City is the famous London Bridge, bought for $2.46 million by Robert P. McCulloch from London, England. The springtime Lake Havasu Regatta boasts the world's largest inland sailing competition. Windsor Beach has a new campground and group camping facility along with two launch ramps. Cattail Cove, 15 miles south, has a campground and boat access campsites. (on Arizona Highway 95 at Havasu City)

Lost Dutchman S.P. is named for one of the most celebrated lost mines in the West. According to legend, German prospector, Jacob Waltz ("The Dutchman") discovered a gold mine in the nearby Superstition Mountains, but died without revealing its location. Maps still circulate, handed down from grandfathers who got them from prospectors who supposedly got them from "The Dutchman." This 292-acre desert park offers camping, picnicking, and trails to the adjacent wilderness area. (5 miles northeast of Apache Junction on Highway 88)

Cheryl Steenerson   LAKE HAVASU STATE PARK

Lyman Lake S.P. is adjacent to a 1,500-acre reservoir on the Little Colorado River. Camping, picnicking, warm-weather water sports, and year-round fishing are popular. (11 miles south of St. John off US Highway 191)

McFarland S.H.P. highlights the political career of Ernest W. McFarland, who held the highest office in each branch of Arizona's government. The original adobe Pinal County Courthouse constructed in 1878-82, are among the architectural interests and related artifacts found here. (in Florence off Highway 287)

Oracle S.P. is a 4,000-acre environmental education park near Oracle in the foothills of the Santa Catalina Mountains. There is access to the scenic Arizona Trail, which will eventually run from Mexico to Utah. (38 miles north of Tucson on Highway 77)

Patagonia Lake S.P. in the Sonoita Valley is one of the most scenic and busiest recreational areas. Water sports, fishing and camping are popular activities. Nearby is the 5,000-acre Sonoita Creek State Natural Area, a unique riparian area featuring giant cottonwoods, willows, mesquites, nesting black hawks and endangered species. (12 miles east of Nogales on Highway 82)

Picacho Peak rises abruptly from the desert floor to a height of 1,500 feet. At this state park, campers and hikers delight in spring wildflowers and desert nature study. (between Phoenix and Tucson on I-10)

Riordan S.H.P. highlights two mansions built in 1904 by Michael and Timothy Riordan and joined by a "rendezvous wing." The Riordans were instrumental in the development of Flagstaff and northern Arizona. (in Flagstaff)

Roper Lake S.P. encircles a fish-rich lake where boating, swimming, camping are available. Nature trails offer a close study of desert plants. (6 miles south of Stafford on US Highway 191)

San Rafael Ranch N.A., offers a historic ranch house, barns, and windmills amid a rolling short-grass prairie. (south of Patagonia, call for directions)

Tombstone Courthouse S.H.P. is a trip back to the turbulent 1880s when Tombstone was known as "the town too tough to die." When prospector Ed Schieffelin went mining for silver, he was warned that all he'd find was Apaches and his tombstone, which is how the town got its name. The Victorian courthouse and the hangman's platform are featured within the park. Surrounding Tombstone offers a variety of historic sites. (in Tombstone)

Tonto Natural Bridge S.P. is the home of the largest natural travertine bridge in the world. Hidden in a small valley surrounded by a pine tree forest, the bridge is 183 feet high above a 400-foot long tunnel that measures 150 feet at its widest point. Several hiking trails descend into pine Canyon below, one of which leads to a cave waterfall. (10 miles north of Payson off Highway 87)

Tubac Presidio S.H.P. presents a mixture of Indian, Spanish, Mexican, and Anglo architectural contributions to the area. Tubac is the oldest town in Arizona, established by people of European descent. (in Tubac)

Yuma Territorial Prison S.H.P. depicts prison life in early Arizona. Perched on a crag overlooking the Colorado River, Yuma tried to foster a sinister reputation: granite cells lined with iron bands, temperatures sometimes reaching 120 degrees, and a rumored "snake pit" dungeon. Famous inmates included mass-murderer Buckskin Frankie Leslie and "Heartless" Pearl Hart, a female stagecoach robber. Present-day exhibits illustrate the convicts, crimes, punishments, and the artifacts that prisoners made and used. (in Yuma)

Yuma Crossing S.H.P. offers a look into Yuma's key role in supplying forts and soldiers during the late 1800s. (1 mile west of the Territorial Prison)

Arizona Office of Tourism   RED ROCK-SEDONA

POINTS OF INTEREST

SEDONA & OAK CREEK CANYON

Sedona is a jewel in the center of the verdant Coconino National Forest, with brilliant red cliffs as its backdrop, 4,300 feet high. A rich cultural center and gateway to the spectacular "Red Rocks Country," it is one of the most popular scenic areas in the state. The town itself was founded in 1902, named after Sedona Miller Schnebly, an early settler. The population now includes many artists and writers. Its center is a parade of galleries which attract art lovers and collectors from afar. Tlaquepaque Arts & Crafts Village replicates its charming namesake, the market square in Old Mexico. The Sedona Art Center, Performing Arts of the Red Rocks, a small theatre, and Red Rock and Slide Rock State Parks further enhance the community. From a distance, Sedona is recognized by its famous landmark— the bell rock—which tops even the tallest trees. At the Sedona Table Top Mountain Airport, planes fly up to land—onto a huge mesa top.

Sedona is 125 miles north of Phoenix and 80 miles south of the Grand Canyon. Situated above the desert heat and below the high altitudes, its climate is moderate year-round. Bird-watching, hiking, and jeep touring are popular with visitors.

The land around Sedona seems to unfold as a paved road follows the stream along the base of the cliffs that comprise

44

Oak Creek Canyon. Its red walls and pinnacles reach to 2,500 feet in some areas, having been cut into Mogollon (MUGGY-own) Rim by Oak Creek.

The canyon is 16 miles long and the lesser side of a mile in width. Colors and patterns on the walls are kaleidoscopic, changing with the sun and shadows as the day progresses. The canyon then opens out into dozens of red rock formations with names like Bell Rock, Merry-go-round, Coffee Pot, Cathedral Rock and Capital Butte. No wonder Oak Creek Canyon has provided the background scenery for many films.

"Red Rock Country" was formed about 320 million years ago (predating dinosaurs by 60 or 70 million years). At that time this area was covered by a vast ocean. When the ocean receded, it left behind deposits of limestone, sandstone, siltstone, and mudstone. The stones layered together in different combinations and were sculpted by wind, rain, and ice. Most resistant to climatic elements, limestone and sandstone emerged as cliffs. Softer siltstone and mudstone tended to wear down into slopes. Six major flat-lying groups of rock resulted, similar to ones 80 miles north in the upper walls of the Grand Canyon. The red coloration comes from an iron oxide mineral which adheres to quartz grains in sandstone and other rocks. Black caps and black vertical columns on many of the groups around Oak Creek Canyon are from intermittent episodes of volcanism occurring from 2.8 million to 200,000 years ago. Molten lava resulted in a covering of basalt, an erosion-resistant substance. For more information, call the Sedona Chamber of Commerce: 928-282-7722.

MUSEUM OF NORTHERN ARIZONA

Located just north of downtown Flagstaff on US Highway 180, this museum has one of the finest collections of Indian art in the southwest. A series of festivals and marketplaces showcasing Native American traditions that have influenced Arizona are held annually May through September. The gift shop offers a wealth of Native American arts and crafts and books on the southwest. Known world-wide for its galleries in archaeology, ethnology, geology, biology, and fine arts, the Museum of Northern Arizona features 40,000 biological specimens, 20,000 fossil, rock and mineral specimens, and more than 2,000 paintings and sculptures—with emphasis on the natural and cultural history of its immediate region: the Colorado Plateau. The Plateau is a major geological province, encompassing parts of Arizona, Utah, Colorado, and New Mexico. Its terrain ranges from alpine tundra and coniferous forests to high

Phoenix & Valley of the Sun CVB   HEARD MUSEUM

deserts. Deep canyons, roaring rivers, mesas, and snow-capped peaks accent the region. 928-774-5213.

THE HEARD MUSEUM

The Heard Museum is an excellent place to experience the southwestern Indian way of life. Navajo weaving, Papago basketry, and Zuni jewelry are on exhibit, along with the Fred Harvey collection of Indian arts and crafts, and the Barry Goldwater collection of Kachinas. Ten exhibit galleries display over 35,000 artifacts. The traditional and contemporary Native American art exhibits are justifiably world renown. Special programs are held throughout the year including the World Championship Hoop Dance Contest and Indian Fair and Market. The Heard Gift Shop is a museum in itself featuring authentic crafts. The museum is located at 2301 North Central Avenue in Phoenix. Contact: www.heard.org and 602-252-8848

PUEBLO GRANDE MUSEUM AND ARCHAEOLOGICAL PARK

Located on the site of a 1,500-year-old Hohokam village, this museum and 102-acre park is dedicated to the culture of the Hohokam people who settled in the Salt River Valley site of present day Phoenix. The park features trails through the ruins, an excavated ball court, and some of the last intact irrigation canals, which are astounding examples of prehistoric engineering. Visitors can experience Hohokam life as they walk through replicas of Hohokam homes, and enjoy a variety of archaeology programs. Near downtown Phoenix: 877-706-4408.

Dick George   DESERT BOTANICAL GARDENS

DESERT BOTANICAL GARDEN

For a taste of nature in the middle of the city, try the Desert Botanical Garden. The Garden boasts the world's largest collection of desert plants in an outdoor setting. More than 10,000 plants and 3,000 different species from all deserts of the world are represented. Two greenhouses feature large displays of exotic cacti. The exhibit trail meanders through a Saguaro forest, mesquite thicket, desert stream environment, and upland chaparral habitat. The Garden's major goal is to educate the public about the fragile balance of the desert and man's ongoing interaction with it. A library, herbarium, lectures, tours, and nature programs relating to desert specimens, history and conservation are offered. The Garden is in Phoenix's Papago Park at 1201 North Galvin Parkway: www.dbg.org or 480-941-1225.

ARIZONA-SONORA DESERT MUSEUM

Calling itself a "living museum," Arizona-Sonora is part zoo, part museum, and part botanical garden. Its purpose is to stress the interrelationships of land, water, plants, wildlife and people of the Sonoran Desert region. Over 400 species of plants and 200 species of animals cohabit on on the museum grounds, designed so that flora and fauna can live as naturally as possible. The Cactus and Succulent Garden showcases 94 species. Visitors use walkways to see animals such as the rare Mexican wolf, river otters, wild cats,

J. Broome   ARIZONA-SONORA DESERT MUSEUM

birds, and other desert critters. The Earth Sciences Center is an underground wonderland of limestone caves.

A community outreach program features regularly scheduled talks, desert ecology classes and field trips to various corners of the Sonoran Desert. "Nighstalking" offers journeys into the desert after dark, when the animals are stirring and the night-blooming cacti are in their glory. "Toadwatch" emphasizes the aquatic animals of the desert in its exploration of temporary rainpools after the summer rains. The Saguaro Harvest Campout is a two-day workshop in harvesting the giant cactus. The fruit is cooked for several hours over mesquite until it thickens into a rich syrup. Papago Indians are on hand to assist and to demonstrate basketmaking. The Museum is adjacent to Saguaro National Park, 14 miles west of Tucson: www.desertmuseum.org or 520-888-2702.